EXPLORING YOUR
INNER SPACE

Exploring Your
INNER SPACE

A *Self-Discovery Journal*

Harry James Cargas

St.
ANTHONY
MESSENGER
PRESS

CINCINNATI, OHIO

for my granddaughters
Nicole Rieder Madden
Madeleine Clark Cargas
*as they begin their
own self-explorations*

Nihil Obstat: Rev. Edward J. Gratsch
Rev. Art Espelage, O.F.M.

Imprimi Potest: Rev. John Bok, O.F.M.
Provincial

Imprimatur: +James H. Garland, V.G.
Archdiocese of Cincinnati
February 8, 1991

Scripture citations are taken from *The New
American Bible With Revised New Testament*,
copyright ©1986 by the Confraternity of
Christian Doctrine, and are used by
permission. All rights reserved.

Cover and book design by Julie Lonneman

ISBN 0-86716-156-6

Published by St. Anthony Messenger Press
Printed in the U.S.A.

Contents

Introduction   1

Part One   9

Journal One
Locating Yourself   11

Journal Two
Reflecting on Your Outer Self   35

Journal Three
Looking Within   83

Journal Four
Probing Spiritual and Moral Issues   97

Journal Five
Dialoguing   119

Journal Six
Imagining the Improbable   135

Part Two   151

Responding to Journal One
Locating Yourself   153

Responding to Journal Two
Reflecting on Your Outer Self   177

Responding to Journal Three
Looking Within   225

Responding to Journal Four
Probing Spiritual and Moral Issues   239

Responding to Journal Five
Dialoguing   261

Responding to Journal Six
Imagining the Improbable   277

Introduction

Space exploration is an adventure open only to a few. But a far more significant journey is available to all of us. The direction of the search is inward. We begin it when we pose the truly meaningful questions of life. We may find some answers if we are willing to take on the spiritual risks of such a journey, risks which can require as much courage as do the physical risks of the astronauts.

Who am I? What does life mean? Does history have a pattern? Answers change as we grow; the important questions stand firm. One such question has to do with the significance of each of us. It may have been nowhere posed better than in this poem by Sweden's Nobel Prize-winning author Par Lagerkvist:

> Like the clouds,
> like a butterfly,
> like the light breathing on a mirror—
>
> Accidental,
> transitory,
> gone in a short while.
>
> Lord over all heavens, all worlds, all fates,
> what have you meant by me?

My life is brief; it occupies a tiny place in the universe. So what has God meant by me?

That is the motivational question behind the questions of this book. In my own search, I look for answers quite different from those of certain philosophers who have decided that my life has

1

precisely the meaning that I give to it. This shallow and basically isolationist view of life cannot take us much beyond a limited outlook—or perhaps "inlook." So I have designed these pages as a guide to searching further for self-discovery, not self-creation.

We Are All Part of a Whole

The more traditional view in Western society, that each of us is part of a whole, that each of us is unique, incomparable and responsible to and for each other, is the lynchpin for the questions in this book. We might benefit from the writer Nikos Kazantzakis' view of himself: "I am the watershed of all of history. I am the culmination of all of the past and the beginning of all of the future." *There* is a man involved in personal adventure! Teilhard de Chardin wrote: Your vocation? To complete the universe.

Nothing less is acceptable to the woman or man who wants to *live*, to achieve the fullest meaning of existence, who refuses to let life just happen. Such people recognize that a far better question than "What do you want to be?" is "Who do you want to become?"

People who want to "become" do not pursue the trivial. Not that they all aim to become senators, Ph.D.'s or headline-makers. They face the challenge to become *themselves*. Socrates taught "Know thy self." Pindar, another Greek of ancient times, said it this way: Become who you are. These four words signify the adventure of each life.

Many American Indians believe that the world is like a giant puzzle. Each of us is a piece in the picture. Some are larger pieces, some smaller. But unless each piece is in place, the picture is incomplete. If I strive to be a larger part of the scene than I have been given to be, I distort it. If I choose to be smaller than I have been given, something will be missing in the picture.

We Must Discover Who We Are

Self-discovery, then, is a double challenge. I am to find out who I am, that is, who God intends me to be, and then live that essence accordingly. Polonius suggests this in *Hamlet* as he advises his son: "This above all: To thine own self be true and it must follow, as the night the day, thou canst not be false to any man."

The questions in this journal-keeping book are designed to help you in the ongoing process of self-discovery. My years of teaching courses in spiritual growth through journal-keeping and of teaching the reading and writing of autobiography inform these pages. The person who faithfully perseveres in the discipline that this self-examination requires may learn much that is satisfying and spirit-enhancing.

This is the kind of book that you can work with more than once. Next year or in three or five or ten years your answers to some or many of these questions will be different. After you have gone through the book again, say in two years, it will be important to your self-understanding to reread what you wrote this year and to compare answers. You will gain insight into your growth.

Each person keeps a journal in an individual manner. There is no "right way" to do it. Some like to write in complete sentences with proper paragraphing and take time to spell each word correctly. Others prefer run-on sentences, no paragraphs and a spelling-be-damned method to keep moving with uninterrupted thought. None of this matters. Honesty is the only absolute criterion. Without honesty the exercises will be not only meaningless but possibly counterproductive.

Perhaps a caution is appropriate here: *honesty* means just that. It does not mean a false humility. The word *humility* is often misunderstood. Humility means recognizing reality as it actually is. If I am poor at something but claim expertise in that activity, I am hardly humble. Likewise, if I am good at something but pretend that I am not, or fail to recognize my competence, that is not humility either. The effort in this exercise (as in all areas of life) is toward humility expressed in truthfulness.

Writing Your Journal

Your journal should be written for your eyes only. Your writing is for self-discovery, not for the information or entertainment of others. Writing for another reader can have a great influence on what you put on paper. Use this time just *for you*!

Date every entry. This will be important when rereading your journal.

Write in ink (or type) so your words will remain readable over a period of time. You may choose to write in this book or in a notebook or elsewhere. Keep the entries together, however. Beware of storing them in a word processor where input can be erased!

A journal is not a diary. A diary is a record of things that you have experienced. The journal is more concerned about the meanings of these experiences. Some overlapping is necessary, but to keep a historical record is far different from interpreting it.

How to Use This Book

This journaling book has two parts. In the first, you will find questions or statements calling for your response. In Part Two you will discover guides to aid you in evaluating your responses. *It is best to begin Part Two only after you have completed all of Part One.* Each entry in Part Two is numbered to correspond with the appropriate entry in Part One. The earlier answer should be read in full immediately before evaluating that answer in Part Two.

Ideally, you should write in your journal on a regular basis. Try to find a time and place each day where you will not be disturbed by children, phone calls, the radio or anything else. A daily encounter with yourself in journaling is the ideal. In this way, you will complete the exercises in the first part of this book in a relatively short time and be able to reflect on your writing while it is still fresh. Adapting to your own schedule, however, is important and it is best to plan how much you can do and follow through rather than go for an ideal which may lead to discouragement.

You are now to embark on interpreting your life. This can be as profound an adventure as you can make it. Take your time with each question. Do not rush. You are worth the pause in daily activity.

You owe it to yourself to learn who you are meant to be. And you owe it to the rest of creation as well.

Become who you are.
Complete the universe.

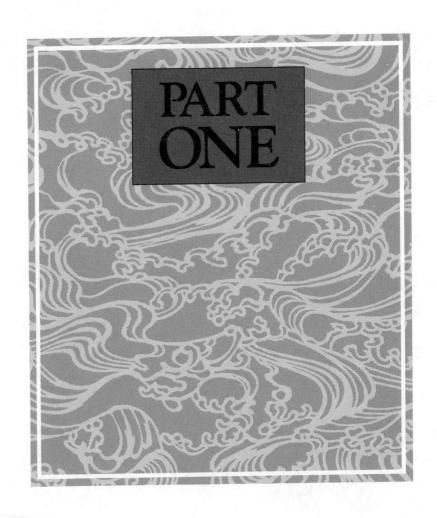

PART ONE

Locating Yourself

In a world frantic for quick answers, it is important to find the right questions. In a society obsessed with hurry, it is imperative to slow down to examine what the race is all about. Many busy people do not even know why they are busy.

Jesus and other spiritual leaders call us to love, compassion, solitude, peace, responsibility and self-development. We cannot respond while we are dashing about at breakneck speed. Slowing down to look at our lives, to pray over them, to seek guidance is necessary to Christian growth. War, economic disaster or environmental mismanagement are not the only things that can destroy us. Lack of purpose, lack of integrity, lack of values can ruin our very selves.

In this first section you will begin by locating yourself, physically, in history and in the universe. Name the specific facts of your existence and condition and think about the paths you have taken to get to where you are in your life-style, family or career. Consider your experiences, preferences, achievements, failures, successes, and the way you see yourself and your life at present.

1. Write down the significant facts of your life; for example, age, sex, ethnic background, health, job, family situations and so on. Be as specific and comprehensive as you can. *Ten minutes.*

DATE _____

2. The line below symbolizes your life span. Put a check mark (√) where you think you are right now on that line.

birth_____death

We desire to do many things in a lifetime. Make a list of things that you think you still have time to do. Draw up another list of things that it may be too late in your life for you to do. *Three minutes.*

3. If you were preparing to write your autobiography, how would you divide the periods of your life? Make a list of the chapter headings for your life story. *Ten minutes.*

4. Give a title to your autobiography. Make it reflect your life as you think it actually is. Next, title your autobiography to reflect the life you wish you were leading. *Three minutes each.*

5. Draw a picture of yourself. *Five minutes.*

6. What is your first memory? *Five minutes.*

7. Tell about the pets you have had. *Eight minutes.*

DATE _____

8. Write about the various hobbies you have (or have had). *Ten minutes.*

9. Tell about your most memorable day. *Five minutes.*

10. Write about how you feel this very moment. *Five minutes.*

11. What do you expect from today? *Five minutes.*

12. Names are important. They imply influence over the destiny of the creature named. Giving oneself a new name is a sign of new realization or new life. Some Afro-Americans have chosen new names (basketball star Lew Alcindor became Kareem Abdul Jabar; poet LeRoi Jones is now Imamu Amiri Baraka). Earlier in this century the vast majority of persons living in Turkey had only one name. A law was passed requiring that each person select a second name.

Choose a new name for yourself. *Three minutes.*

13. If you could choose to be any animal, bird or fish, what creature would you choose to be? *Three minutes.*

DATE _____

4. Which of your possessions gives you the greatest pleasure? *Five minutes.*

15. What do you like to do for sheer joy? *Five minutes.*

6. Whom do you want to impress? Why? *Five minutes.*

17. Finish the following sentence and then explain your choice. "The favorite part of my house is...." *Five minutes.*

DATE _____

8. List the TV programs you most frequently watch. How regularly do you see them? *Four minutes.*

19. What is your favorite song or musical work? What makes it so special for you? *Five minutes.*

DATE _____

20. In general, do you like most of the people you meet? Write the names of some of the people you have met in the past two or three weeks. *Ten minutes.*

DATE _____

21.
Would you say that you have enough friends? Why or why not?
Ten minutes.

22. In Japan, Naikan psychotherapists ask their clients to concentrate on the gratitude that they owe to people who have helped them become what they are and to achieve what they have achieved. Do that for yourself. List the people to whom you feel you owe a personal debt of thanks. Tell how it is that each of them aided you. *20 minutes.*

Journal Two

Reflecting on Your Outer Self

Now that you have named some of the facts and situations of your life, begin to look at your "outer self." Consider the face you show to the world, the face which sometimes masks the real you and at other times reveals the true person that you are.

So often people fear self-discovery—it seems to have negative connotations. Yet men and women who pursue it are frequently surprised to find out positive aspects of themselves of which they were unaware. So the point of the questions that follow, like all of the exercises in this book, is to assist you in learning more about the real you.

As you take a long look at your outer self, try to come to a greater understanding of your personality and your purpose.

DATE _____

1. Words have significance in each of our lives; for instance, love, freedom, father, job, home, fear. Try to discover the key words for your life. Write as many as you can. *12 minutes.*

DATE _____

2. Make a list of your positive qualities.

Make a list of your negative qualities. *Five minutes each.*

3. Sometimes we overlook or take for granted our own best skills and talents. Below give an honest and comprehensive summary of your skills and talents. Explain each of them, briefly or at length. *12 minutes.*

4. Make a list of characteristics of your public self, that is, how you think you are seen by others. Draw up a second list of characteristics of your private self, characteristics you think that others seldom see. *Eight minutes.*

5. What have you done that you are most proud of? Explain. *Six minutes.*

6. What is the best advice you have ever received? How have you responded to that advice? *Seven minutes.*

7. If you could receive one gift, what would you like it to be? Explain your choice. *Seven minutes.*

8. Who are your heroes? Why? Who are your villains? Why? *Ten minutes each.*

DATE _____

9. What one word best describes you? Why is this the best word? *Five minutes.*

10. List criticisms that you have received.

List compliments which have been given to you. *Five minutes each.*

11. If you could relive one day in your life, which day would you select? Tell why. *Eight minutes.*

2. With which events or circumstances in your life have you yet to make peace? *Five minutes.*

13. What would it take to make you as happy as possible? *Five minutes.*

DATE _____

4. How much control do you feel you exercise over your life? *Eight minutes.*

15. Complete the following sentence: What I need now in my life is....
Five minutes.

6. Some people see work as a curse, a punishment for sin. Others look upon work as an opportunity for fulfillment. Some men and women find only drudgery in work. Some see it as a natural part of life and don't give much thought to any philosophy of work. How do you regard work (not your job in particular, but work in general)? *Ten minutes.*

DATE _____

17. What is the most difficult thing you have ever accomplished? (There may be two answers here, one accomplishment that took a relatively long time to achieve and one which required less time or effort.) *Five minutes each.*

8. In his autobiography *Scattered Shadows*, John Howard Griffin tells of his gradual loss of sight and of how he made preparations to live as a blind man. If you had just two more weeks to see, what images would you store during that time? *Ten minutes.*

19. How do you feel right now? *Five minutes.*

20. If you knew you were close to death, what advice would you leave for those who are to come after you? *Seven minutes.*

DATE _____

21. Would you like to become famous? If so, what would you like to be noted for? If not, why not? *Six minutes.*

DATE _____

2. In what situation(s) do you feel pressure? Should you change the situation(s)? If so, how? *Ten minutes.*

23. On one hand, wasting time can be a way of sidestepping responsibilities. On the other hand, as psychologists and spiritual authorities indicate, wasting some time may be healthy, necessary and an important change of pace. In what ways do you waste time? How often? Do you consider this time well spent or truly wasted? *Eight minutes.*

4. Do you like yourself? Why or why not? *Ten minutes.*

DATE _____

25. If you could receive an award, what would you like it to be for? *Five minutes.*

DATE _____

26. List some things that make you angry. After each, write down why they do. *Six minutes.*

27. St. Basil, writing of both uniqueness and responsibility, asked this rhetorical question: "Are you not a thief if you keep for your own what has been given to you for dispensing and sharing?" Discuss which gift(s) you may have that you might develop and share with others. *Ten minutes.*

28. Everyone encounters many crises in life. We can be shattered by them. Or we might grow from them. List some of the crises you have gone through and write your reaction to each. You might want to consider how you responded at the time they occurred and how you would deal with each of those events now. *15 minutes.*

29. What do you most look forward to in the future? Explain your response. *Ten minutes.*

30. If you could add several people to your family, who would they be? Why have you listed these particular persons? *Eight minutes.*

31. Complete this sentence: If I could live any place I wanted to in the world, I would choose.... Give reasons for your answer. *Five minutes.*

32. If you could invite any three persons, living or dead, to a dinner party at your house, whom would you ask? Why them? *Seven minutes.*

33. Outline what you would consider a great vacation. *Five minutes.*

34. If you could have any job in the world, what would you choose to do? *Five minutes.*

35. What would you like to be doing in three years? *Eight minutes.*

36. Write about the best job (or class) that you have ever had. Why is this one the best? *Seven minutes.*

37. Who has been your greatest teacher *outside of the classroom*? What did this person teach you of great importance? *Eight minutes.*

38. What are the main qualifications that you look for in a friend? Why are these attributes important to you? *Eight minutes.*

DATE _____

39. Is it more usual for you to praise another person or to be critical? Why? *Ten minutes.*

40. Complete this sentence: One thing I missed in my childhood was....
Five minutes.

41. Describe your ideal of good sportsmanship. *Five minutes.*

DATE _____

42. What do you do best? Why? *Seven minutes.*

DATE _____

43. How would you rate yourself if you were asked how frequently you flirt? (a) quite frequently (b) sometimes (c) occasionally (d) rarely (e) never. *Two minutes.*

4. We often overlook the richness of life that comes through our five senses of sight, hearing, touch, smell and taste. Take the time now to talk to each of them. Tell what each means to you, how each has helped you, possibly how one or several have disappointed you. Perhaps you wish to write something regarding your failure to appreciate one or more of your senses. You may even resolve how to develop a better "relationship" with one (or several) that you realize you may have neglected. *30 minutes.*

45. When was the last time you cried? What were the circumstances?
Seven minutes.

DATE _____

6. What does your country mean to you? *Ten minutes.*

DATE _____

47. When you are angry, how do you think you look? *Five minutes.*

Journal Three

Looking Within

Everyone's life matters. In what way(s) does yours have significance? No life is meaningless. In what ways is yours meaningful? In which areas can you do better, *be* better? Are you directing the course of your life? Or are you just letting it happen to you? Christianity is, after all, a call to heroism, to heroic living. Heroism does not imply physical courage or famous achievements. It has to do with living with love, honor, integrity, principle and other similar virtues. It has to do with rising up again and again from the ashes of failure, of challenging life anew instead of giving in to despair, of getting up and going on after we are knocked down.

It is time to turn inward, to look for your less obvious characteristics. Honest reflection is crucial. Of course, you are not writing answers for anyone else to read. And you do not need to hurry your responses. So you can take your time, reflect and learn from this great adventure into your self.

Become more aware of your uniqueness; recognize your many good qualities; take into account your shortcomings. This will help to strengthen areas you are already developing and to improve parts of your personality that need attention. If you can, call yourself to look at any aspects of your life which you have been avoiding or afraid to face.

Just as it takes courage to live, so too it takes courage to reflect on living. The results of doing so can be of ultimate value.

DATE _____

1. What do you think is the meaning of life? Do you need to change anything in order to come into greater harmony with your life's purpose? *30 minutes.*

DATE _____

2. Some people set goals about what they want to do in life. Others emphasize how they want to live rather than what they want to do. Some care more about *doing*, others about *being*. How do see your life best fulfilled? To help you to answer this, use a technique suggested by Viktor Frankl, the Austrian psychiatrist who founded an intriguing system called logotherapy. Project yourself forward in time and imagine yourself on your deathbed. Look back on your life and write about how or who it is you wish you could have *been* and what it is you wish you could have *done. 25 minutes.*

3. Write your last will and testament. Leave your possessions to whomever you wish. As part of this document, make an ethical will: Tell those who are important to you what you would like to say to them. Make it a kind of love letter from life beyond. *25 minutes.*

DATE _____

4. What would you like to change most about yourself? Why would you want to make the change? *Seven minutes.*

5. What kinds of things do you do when you are alone and no one is watching you? *Five minutes.*

6. When your mind wanders or during the time just before you fall asleep, what generally comes to your mind? *Five minutes.*

7. What are you ashamed of? Can you give reasons for your feelings? *Seven minutes.*

8. Of whom or what are you suspicious? *Seven minutes.*

9. What do you fear most? Why? *Seven minutes.*

0. How do you feel at this moment? *Five minutes.*

DATE _____

11. Elaborate on this sentence: I do (not) have time for myself. *Five minutes.*

2.

What causes you to feel most lonely? *Five minutes.*

DATE _____

13. What are some of the areas of tension in your life? Think about home, personal relations, health, religion, money, sexuality, work or school, particular persons or any other areas where there may be significant discontent. *15 minutes.*

Probing Spiritual and Moral Issues

This section brings you face-to-face with the kinds of experiences, conflicts and questions that thoughtful people have been pondering for centuries: questions of spirituality, suffering, evil, aggression, morality, sexuality and so on. Philosophers, theologians, psychologists and educators have addressed these topics. Each of us, too, can profit from clarifying our thinking about them.

DATE _____

1. Describe the most religious or spiritual experience that you have ever had. *Seven minutes.*

2. If you had 20 minutes to speak with Jesus, Moses, Mary, Mohammed, the Buddha or a comparable religious figure, whom would you choose? What would you ask that person? What would you tell him or her? *20 minutes.*

DATE_____

3. Write on the topic of *evil*. (What is it? Where does it come from? Give some examples.) *Ten minutes.*

4. Explain to someone what you mean by serving God. *Ten minutes.*

DATE_____

5. What are your honest feelings about God? About religion? How have your feelings about God and religion had an impact on your life? *15 minutes.*

6. Do you believe in an afterlife? If you do, what form do you think it will take? *Ten minutes.*

7. If transmigration of souls or reincarnation were a fact, in what form—or in what place or under what circumstances—would you like to return to earth in your next life? Be as specific as possible. *Six minutes.*

8. Write down your thoughts and feelings about death. *Ten minutes.*

9. Are you superstitious? About what and why? *Seven minutes.*

10. About what things are you dishonest? Why? *Six minutes.*

11. What is your greatest hope? For yourself? For the people closest to you? For the world? Explain your answers. *Seven minutes.*

2. What things come to your mind about war? How do you define war: Must it be an international conflagration or may it be considerably more limited? Do you think war is ever justified? If so, under what circumstances? *Ten minutes.*

DATE_____

13. Do you have a code or certain ideals regarding your own personal sexuality? If so, what is included in it? Consider whether you regard sexual union a serious matter or something casual. Consider how you feel about premarital sexuality. *15 minutes.*

4. Would you say that you tend to regard your (potential) sex partner fully as a person or more as an object for your own gratification—or perhaps somewhere between those two poles? *Seven minutes.*

15. How do you feel about couples who are not married living together? *Six minutes.*

DATE_____

6. Do you tell jokes about sex? Do you like to hear them? *Three minutes.*

17. Is adultery acceptable to you: (a) in most circumstances, (b) sometimes or (c) never? *Eight minutes.*

8. How would you feel if you learned that your parents were not faithful to each other? Or if your children lived promiscuously? *Ten minutes.*

DATE_____

19. What are your thoughts on homosexuality and individuals who are homosexually active? *Ten minutes.*

DATE_____

0. Overall, do you think that your approach to sexuality is a healthy one? *15 minutes.*

21. What do you think that the world needs now? How might the world obtain it? *Ten minutes.*

Journal Five

Dialoguing

As you know, a dialogue involves two or more people speaking to each other. In this section you will dialogue on paper with some people of your choosing. You will also be invited to hold some dialogues with yourself.

Discussing significant ideas with significant men and women through fantasy can prove both gratifying and instructive—as well as fun. Take this opportunity to allow your imagination to romp, to take chances, to discover, to help yourself to grow.

Dialogues completed often move us to action. Talking about goodness is of importance; being good is of far greater value. Extolling integrity, humility, hope and prayerfulness cannot compare with being honorable, humble, hopeful and prayerful. We all know people who insist, "Don't do as I do, do as I say." But if we do not ratify what we say by what we do, who can have confidence in our words or our selves?

Is the quality of your life to be found in your actions or in your advice? As the observation goes, words can be pretty cheap. Good lives, on the other hand, are great treasures. Though none of us will ever be perfect, we can each strive toward the ideal life to which we feel called.

1. Write a letter to someone you have never met. Tell that person about yourself. Include your appearance, background, interests, concerns, hobbies, activities and so on. *15 minutes.*

2. Who is your greatest hero or role model? Imagine that this person is with you now. Discuss a subject that is important to you with that person. Do this as a dialogue, writing your words and the other person's responses. *Ten minutes.*

3. Choose a contemporary public figure and write a letter telling that person exactly what you want to say to him or her. *Seven minutes.*

4. Hold a conversation with someone from the past: Napoleon, Socrates, a matron from the Roman Empire, Marco Polo, Catherine of Siena, a student from the Middle Ages, Helen of Troy, a pre-Civil War slave, Martin Luther, a 14th-century camel driver, a woman who went west in the pioneer wagons or anyone of your choosing. You might even wish to speak with more than one historical figure. Write your dialogues. *Ten to 15 minutes each.*

DATE _____

5. Write an imaginary discussion with a good friend. *Ten minutes.*

DATE _____

6. Write a talk that might take place between you and someone you dislike a good deal. The person may be part of your present or your past. *Ten minutes.*

7. Choose any three key words that you listed in entry 1 in Journal 2 (page 34). Dialogue with each of those words. *Five to ten minutes each.*

8. Create a dialogue between the person you are now and the person you were ten years ago. *Ten minutes.*

9. Create a dialogue between the person you are now and the person you will be ten years from now. *Ten minutes.*

0. If God appeared to you at this moment, record how you think a conversation might go. *15 minutes.*

DATE _____

11. Dialogue with a present or past boss or teacher. *Ten minutes.*

12. Imagine a dialogue with your body. What would be said?
Five minutes.

13. Write a dialogue with one or both of your parents (living or deceased). *15 minutes.*

14. Write a conversation you would like to have with your (real or imaginary) spouse. *Ten minutes.*

DATE _____

15. Write a love letter to yourself. Take plenty of time; you are worth it.

Imagining Possibilities

These questions challenge you to imagine what life could be like for you or what you would do if circumstances in your life changed.

1. Suppose someone just gave you $5 million. What would you do with it? *Ten minutes.*

2. If you were to become instantly poverty-stricken, what would you do first? *Seven minutes.*

3. Tell somebody off. Do not be afraid of using harsh language here. *Five minutes.*

4. If you learned that you had exactly one week to live, how would you behave that week? *Ten minutes.*

5. How might you improve the work (or study) part of your life? *Ten minutes.*

DATE _____

6. What would make your family life better? *Ten minutes.*

DATE _____

7. There are fairy tales about characters earning special wishes which are guaranteed to come true. If you had the opportunity to have three wishes granted, what could they be? *Five minutes.*

8. In what ways could you simplify your life? *Ten minutes.*

9. What is the worst thing that parents can do to children? *Seven minutes.*

70. What is the best thing that parents can do for children? *Seven minutes.*

11. Imagine yourself successful to the highest degree. Describe your life. *Ten minutes.*

2. Some persons have values for which they are willing to die. Is there anything for which you are willing to die? *Five minutes.*

DATE _____

13. As a follow-up to the previous entry, indicate the values for which you are eager to live. *Five minutes.*

4. Describe peace. *Four minutes.*

15. What are you feeling right now? *Three minutes.*

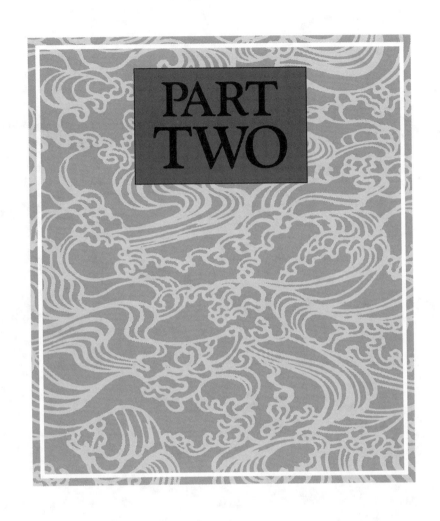

PART
TWO

Reflections on Journal One

Locating Yourself

1. Check your answers to see what kinds of things you emphasized. Did you start with the items given as examples in the instruction or with some other aspects of yourself? Did you elaborate on certain parts but not others? What facts did you leave out: for example, your weight, skills, shortcomings, education, geographic location, strong points, height? Did you deliberately omit certain things or perhaps leave them out subconsciously? Did you leave some things out because they are not important to you? Is there anything you would add now? *Refer to page 10.*

2. Look over the "too late" category again. Is the label "too late" realistic or pessimistic? Do you see any items you could transfer to the other column? Concentrate on the things you do have time for and write how you think that you might go about doing them. Perhaps you might rank them in order of priority and then see which entries on your list you want to accomplish first. *Refer to page 11.*

3. How did you approach this: chronologically, by achievements, happy recollections, sad memories, various moves, schools, jobs? What does this tell you about your attitude toward your life? *Refer to page 12.*

4. Discuss any differences(s) between the two titles that you selected for your autobiography. What would it take for you to "realize" the preferred title? *Refer to page 13.*

5. What have you emphasized and what have you overlooked in drawing yourself? For instance, did you concentrate on one portion of your body? If so, why? Have you underplayed any part of your appearance? What does that tell you? Have you stressed parts of your anatomy of which you are particularly proud or especially displeased? Are you smiling, looking directly forward, in action, at rest? Have you drawn yourself rather large or small? What kind of clothing is on your drawing? Can you give reasons for any of this? *Refer to page 14.*

6. How old were you during this memory? Should you be able to think farther back? If so, are you, perhaps, blocking a memory? *Refer to page 15.*

7. Do you generally recall happy times with your pets or such times as when your dog bit you, your canary died, your cat tore the curtains? Were pets an important part of your life? *Refer to page 16.*

8. Were (are) hobbies fun for you or do they have a way of becoming obsessions? Do you participate regularly, irregularly, competitively, with great joy or little satisfaction? Do you try mainly to achieve or to enjoy? *Refer to page 17.*

9. Was it a day of joy, or tragedy, or accomplishment, pain or failure? Do you have a tendency to dwell on *doing* or *being*? Do your recollections tend toward the happy or the less happy occasions? *Refer to page 18.*

0. Were you happy, sad, tense, puzzled? Was this a common feeling or was it exceptional? Explain. How do you feel at this moment? *Refer to page 19.*

11. Would you say your expectations are high, low, average? Does this represent your general attitude toward life? *Refer to page 20.*

DATE_____

2. Did you select a name of beauty, power, humor, honor? What does your choice say about your way of thinking about yourself? *Refer to page 21.*

13. What kind of creature did you choose? Is it one of delicacy, speed, power, grace, insignificance? Is it one that somehow parallels certain characteristics of your actual self? Is it completely different from the way you see yourself? *Refer to page 22.*

DATE_____

4. Reflect on the kinds of possessions you chose. Are they showy? For self-satisfaction? Are they items to share or to keep to yourself? Would they be of value to others? *Refer to page 23.*

15. Is this something you do by yourself or with others? Do you like to tell people about this activity or keep it private? Would you suggest that others among your family and friends do the same? *Refer to page 24.*

6. Some want to impress a loved one; others, a boss. You may have chosen God. Or someone who can make you famous or do you "some good." You may even have selected yourself. Whatever your answer, what does it say about you? *Refer to page 25.*

DATE_____

17. Have you selected a place with happy memories? A site where you can be alone? Perhaps you picked an area where the family gathers, a room with much sunlight during the day or a place free from noise. Does your choice reveal anything about yourself? *Refer to page 26.*

DATE_____

8. There are two parts to this answer, the *what* and the *how often*. Do you generally watch programs for information, entertainment, escape, or just to have some "company" in your life? How do you decide what and when you watch? What benefits do you get from watching TV? Does your watching ever prevent you from doing more fruitful activities? *Refer to page 27.*

19. Is the song associated with a memory? Is it lovely in itself? Is it a relatively recent favorite or have you enjoyed it for quite a while? Does it have a message? (If so, what is the message?) Are values reflected here that indicate something revealing about your values? *Refer to page 28.*

20. Do you make it easy or difficult for someone to get to know you? Are you initially trusting or suspicious of others? Does everyone have an equal chance with you or are some types less welcome? Is the way you are the way you wish to be? *Refer to page 29.*

21. Do you find yourself actively seeking friends? Or are you easygoing, making friends or not as the situations develop? *Refer to page 30.*

22. Think again about people who helped you. Did you consider traditional people like parents, teachers, aunts, uncles, sisters, brothers and so on? What of neighbors, authors, news makers, historical figures, relative strangers you have encountered just once? Are there similarities or great differences among them? Are their approaches to life of a particular pattern? What values did they represent to you? *Refer to page 31.*

Reflecting on Your Outer Self

DATE_____

1. Is there a pattern to the words you listed? For example, did you list many words that signify happiness, pain, power, insecurity, fear, hope? Below are some words you may have omitted. Did you leave them off your list because they are not that important to you or for other reasons? If you would like to add any of these words to your list, do so now. *Refer to page 34.*

parent(s)	car	dog	creative
money	clothing	bored	spouse
recreation (play)	death	achievement	success
order	peace	fun (laughter)	music
sex	God	Bible	nature
time	war	enjoyment	feminine
freedom	art	school	masculine
secret	mean	sleep	books
hatred	alone	tolerance	risk
work	assault	business	politics
politics	children	energy	travel
foreigner	friendship	change	prayer
water	drugs	search	loyalty
television	share	alcohol	balance
food	growth	silence	independence
education	insanity	dream	progress
fire	responsibility	efficient	surrender
adventure	sad	church	kind
birth	trust	past	people
health	service	ugly	news
neighbor(s)	commitment	beauty	intimacy
weight	tension	control	divorce
ego	truth	values	perseverance
power	snow	grandparent(s)	open
goal	future	communicating	holiday(s)
emotions	culture	home	clean

2. Do your positive attributes outweigh the negative? What steps can you take to build on the positives and try to minimize the negatives? *Refer to page 35.*

DATE_____

3. Do you do many things well or a few things well? How do you wish to use these skills? Are there any that you wish to improve upon? *Refer to page 36.*

4. What image of yourself do you prefer—the one you show to the public or the one you keep private? Would the *ideal* you be a combination of the two? *Refer to page 37.*

5. How do these acts reflect your values or standards? *Refer to page 38.*

6. Was the advice geared toward financial or social success? Or toward how to live a full or happy life? How has this advice helped you? *Refer to page 39.*

7. What is the nature of this gift? Does your wish tell something about who you are? *Refer to page 40.*

DATE_____

8. Are your heroes important to you because they do great things, because they are popular, because they are comfortable with themselves? Or because they are rich, holy, attractive, humorous? Are your villains the opposite of your heroes? *Refer to page 41.*

9. Is this word consistent with who you think you are? With who you wish to be? *Refer to page 42.*

DATE_____

0. Evaluate both the compliments and the criticisms you have received. Did you list far more in one category than the other? Are the criticisms and/or the compliments accurate? Are you the best judge? How do you react to criticism? To a compliment? How truthfully do you criticize and compliment yourself? *Refer to page 43.*

11. Was this a day of achievement, recognition, relaxation, love? Does the kind of day you picked tell something about your personality? *Refer to page 44.*

2. How can you bring about peace with these events? Do you actually want to make peace with each of them (people or situations)? *Refer to page 45.*

13. Evaluate your response. Would you say it is somewhat selfish, fulfilling, thoughtful, impossible? *Refer to page 46.*

DATE_____

4. Do you feel life is almost totally out of your control or that you are in charge of just about everything? How realistic are you? Would you be better off trying to exercise more control or less? *Refer to page 47.*

15. Does your answer show your need for material things, health, spiritual growth? Is this a reflection of your deepest self? *Refer to page 48.*

6. Is work satisfying for you? What influence do your thoughts about work have on your life-style? Would you like to change your idea of the nature of work or is it comfortable to you? *Refer to page 49.*

DATE_____

17. The techniques and discipline that you employed to achieve success(es) here may tell something about your character. Discuss that now. Also, write about how you might adapt these ways to other works you would like to accomplish. *Refer to page 50.*

8. Which kinds of images do you try to store: of people, the little things you love, nature, famed sites? Does this reveal anything about your values? *Refer to page 51.*

19. Is this typical of the way you usually feel? How do you feel right now? *Refer to page 52.*

0. Is this advice of a more spiritual or more materialistic nature? Did you write out of anger, disappointment, happiness? *Refer to page 53.*

21. Discuss the value or drawbacks of fame. *Refer to page 54.*

2. Are you overwhelmed by certain pressures? Are they significant in your life? Are the ways you have suggested to ease the pressures realistic? Should you meet the problems head on or sidestep them? Which would be best for you? *Refer to page 55.*

23. Do you waste too much time? Not enough? Do the ways in which you do so cause embarrassment or can you recommend them to others? *Refer to page 56.*

DATE_____

24. This is an important question. Are the reasons for your answer adequate? If you do not like yourself, check to see if your answers show that you fail to recognize your true value. *Refer to page 57.*

25.
What kind of award did you name? Was it for service to others, personal achievement, beauty, fame? Was it for something that you are doing now or hope to do soon? Or was it for something completely different from anything you are now prepared to do? *Refer to page 58.*

DATE_____

26. Do you wish to cut down on your anger—or do you need to own it more fully? How might you begin? *Refer to page 59.*

27. If you did not discuss *how* you might implement the sharing of your gifts in your response, do so here. *Refer to page 60.*

28. Is there a pattern to the way you have reacted to crisis situations in your life? Are you calm under pressure or do you tend to become confused? Have you grown because of certain crises or do they tend to bring your life to a standstill? *Refer to page 61.*

29. In your answer, did you concentrate more on your *doing* or your *being*? Were you concerned primarily with a life of integrity? Did the judgments of others sometimes enter into your considerations? Does your life now indicate in some ways that you are moving in a direction appropriate to some of the goals you would like to achieve? How can you adjust your life, realistically, to help you toward those ends? *Refer to page 62.*

30. How do the people that you selected "fit in" with your family now? Did you choose them because they can bring something special into your family? Would you be content to have them as family members 20 years from now? Why or why not? *Refer to page 63.*

31. Have you selected a place for escape, involvement, peace, the environment, to be near certain persons? Think also about what kinds of places you would not like to live in. What are your major concerns? *Refer to page 64.*

DATE_____

2. On what bases did you select these persons? Are they all from the same field? All men or all women? From various ethnic backgrounds? How does your choice of these people tell about you and your values? *Refer to page 65.*

33. How close have you come to such an ideal vacation? Can you do something to make it a possibility? *Refer to page 66.*

34. Are you now qualified for such a position, or can you become qualified? Is it realistic for you to want to do this? How can you make your present work more satisfying, more fulfilling? *Refer to page 67.*

35. Is the response here about something that is likely to happen or is it too "dreamy"? Is it about something that will benefit only you or others also? Try to evaluate your answer in relation to your overall personality. *Refer to page 68.*

DATE_____

36. Write about the worst class or job you have experienced. Discuss the contrast between this worst one and your choice as the best one. *Refer to page 69.*

37. Does your choice tell you something about how you learn? What characteristics do you admire most in the person you cited in your answer? *Refer to page 70.*

8. How do you try to cultivate the qualifications in yourself as a friend to someone else? *Refer to page 71.*

39. Does your response indicate anything about your style, your ego, your feelings of superiority or inferiority? If so, what? *Refer to page 72.*

Q. Are you bitter about this? Self-pitying? Accepting? How do you
think you might be different if you had not missed this "one thing"?
Refer to page 73.

41. Is good sportsmanship generally practiced in your milieu? Can it be improved? Can you be considered a good sport? *Refer to page 74.*

DATE_____

2. Was it difficult to answer this question because you do many things well? Or do you do a few things with distinction? Or do you have a hard time recognizing your gifts and skills? What does this indicate about your attitude toward yourself? *Refer to page 75.*

43. Do you feel that flirting is harmless? What purpose does it serve? *Refer to page 76.*

4. Which sense(s) have you emphasized? Which have you slighted? Check to see if you are losing any important aspects of living because you are neglecting the development of certain senses. *Refer to page 77.*

45. Do you cry too easily or too rarely? Are you embarrassed or ashamed to weep? In general, do you regard your emotions as honest? *Refer to page 78.*

6. Are you a superpatriot? Or one who is very much down on your country? Or indifferent? Are you satisfied with your attitude? Why or why not? *Refer to page 79.*

47. How do you feel about your anger? *Refer to page 80.*

Reflections on Journal Three

Looking Within

1. Has it been a regular practice of yours to reflect on the meaning of life? What does your answer about this practice say about who you are, about how you live your life? Do you consider it important to think about the purposes and goals of the universe or is it all too difficult, too impossible, too frustrating? Again, how does this show who you are? *Refer to page 82.*

2. Did you concentrate more on your *doing* or your *being*? Were you concerned primarily with a life of integrity or did how others would judge you enter your consideration? Does your life now indicate in some way that you are moving in a direction appropriate to some of the goals you would like to achieve? How can you adjust your life to help you toward those ends? *Refer to page 83.*

3. How do you feel about writing an ethical will? If you could send one to as many persons as you wish, to whom would you do so? *Refer to page 84.*

DATE_____

4. Are there actual steps that you can take to effect the changes you want? Are you willing to take them? *Refer to page 85.*

DATE_____

5. Consider what your answer says about your life. *Refer to page 86.*

DATE_____

6. Are these thoughts worrisome, sexual, self-centered, relaxing, prayerful? Elaborate. *Refer to page 87.*

7. How does this answer reveal a facet of your values? *Refer to page 88.*

8. Are your reasons justified? Is it your habit to be generally suspicious? Are you overly suspicious? Overly trusting? *Refer to page 89.*

DATE_____

9. Is this different from your suspicions? Is there something that you can do to lessen your fear? *Refer to page 90.*

0. Is your mood representative of how you usually are? What are you feeling right now? *Refer to page 91.*

11. Does your answer reflect how you regard yourself? Are you satisfied with "your relationship with you"? If you feel you should develop this relationship, how might you go about it? *Refer to page 92.*

2. Being alone, of course, is not the same as being lonely. Why do you think you do feel lonely at certain times (if you do)? If loneliness is a problem, can you do anything about it? *Refer to page 93.*

13. This is an important "action" question. What specific actions can you take to relieve the various tensions that trouble you? *Refer to page 94.*

Probing Spiritual and Moral Issues

1. Did this experience have an impact on your life? If so, what impact did it have? Have you had other spiritual experiences? *Refer to page 96.*

2. What did you talk about? Did you express to the religious figure how you feel about him or her? Did the things you talked about show more concern for others or yourself? *Refer to page 97.*

3. Did you consider evil in broad, world-effecting terms or from a personal perspective? Did Satan or other figures enter your discussion? Did you consider individual responsibility? Did you mention sin? Why or why not? *Refer to page 98.*

4. How have you framed this explanation: in personal terms, in some fear, in ambiguity, in traditional ways? What can you say about your attitude toward religion? *Refer to page 99.*

DATE_____

5. Write about how you felt in answering this question honestly. Was it difficult, awkward or quite comfortable? Can you say something about the future of your relationship with God? *Refer to page 100.*

6. Do you see an afterlife as a reward/punishment kind of existence? Is it a threat, a comfort, fulfilling in some way or another step in a process? *Refer to page 101.*

7. How does your answer reflect your sense of the future or ideas about the interconnectedness of all life? What does it say about your needs and desires? *Refer to page 102.*

DATE_____

8. How did you approach this topic, as a general subject or from the way it affects your personality? Did you emphasize loss, nothingness, pain, fulfillment, hope? *Refer to page 103.*

9. What does your answer indicate about your personality, your religious beliefs, your fear or lack of fear? *Refer to page 104.*

DATE_____

0. Can you rationalize your dishonesty or is it just plain wrong?
Should you remedy your ways in this matter? *Refer to page 105.*

11. What type was your hope: spiritual, material, relational? What does your answer imply about your values? *Refer to page 106.*

2. Have you written about war in general or in its relation to its impact on you? Can wars ever be eliminated? *Refer to page 107.*

13.

Does your answer have a basis in moral, societal and religious values? *Refer to page 108.*

4. Can you evaluate, through the response that you gave, whether your attitude is more selfless or selfish? *Refer to page 109.*

15. On what principle(s) did you base your answer? *Refer to page 110.*

DATE_____

6. Why do you think that sex jokes are popular? What values do they imply? *Refer to page 111.*

17.

What are the standards inherent in your answers? *Refer to page 112.*

DATE_____

8. Do you have different standards for your parents and your children than you have for yourself when it comes to sexuality? If you do, explain your attitude. *Refer to page 113.*

19.

On what grounds did you base your responses? *Refer to page 114.*

DATE_____

Q. What constitutes healthy sexuality? How does your behavior compare with the standards that you feel are ideal? *Refer to page 115.*

21.
Can you do something to help fill this need? How should you proceed? *Refer to page 116.*

Dialoguing

1. What kinds of things did you choose to tell? What did you opt to leave out? Judge your letter. Is it reasonably modest? Honest about yourself? Is it bragging about yourself? *Refer to page 118.*

2. Did you discuss the topic most pertinent to you or did you match your subject with the person? Explain. Why that topic? *Refer to page 119.*

DATE_____

3. Did you first select the individual and then the topic or vice-versa? Why that particular subject? *Refer to page 120.*

4. On what basis did you choose the historic person? Did your discussion center more on him or her or on yourself? What tone did you use (formal, conversational, glib, angry, reverential)? Why? *Refer to page 121.*

DATE_____

5. Why this friend, why that subject? Did you give your friend a fair representation in the discussion? Were you fair to yourself? Elaborate. *Refer to page 122.*

6. Why did you choose this person from all others? Did you try to portray the other's viewpoint adequately in the dialogue? Is there something you can learn from your adversary? Was the mood of this discussion one that might lead to reconciliation or was it quite the contrary? *Refer to page 123.*

7. Can you explain why you used those three words and not any of the others? Was it because they are pleasant, puzzling, frightening, nonthreatening, stimulating? Did you deliberately bypass certain words? *Refer to page 124.*

8. What are the major differences in you between now and then? Are you generally pleased with your growth? Are you happy with the way you were then? *Refer to page 125.*

9. What leads you to think that you will be like that in ten years? *Refer to page 126.*

0. Consider the topics you talked about. Did you ask for things for yourself and others? Was the dialogue awkward? Why or why not? *Refer to page 127.*

DATE_____

11. Was this a friendly conversation or one between adversaries? Did you remember the humanity of the other person or was it more the role of that person to which you tried to relate? *Refer to page 128.*

2. How do you regard your body: Is it a part of yourself? Separate from yourself? Or is your body *you* (in the sense that you *are* your body just as you *are* your mind—as opposed to *having* a body and *having* a mind)? Does your response say anything of significance regarding your attitude toward yourself? *Refer to page 129.*

13. What is your attitude toward your parents? Is it "justified" in the light of your relationship? Are you able to keep your father and mother distinct and not lump them under the single heading "parents"? How do you feel about your attitude toward your parents? *Refer to page 130.*

4. What important values have you expressed about marriage in general, about your marriage in particular, about the person you are linked with in this exercise? *Refer to page 131.*

15. Was this difficult or awkward? Do you believe that you are worth such an effort? Or was this "too easy" because in certain ways you really are "stuck on yourself"? What kinds of things did you emphasize? What kinds of values do they suggest? *Refer to page 132.*

Imagining Possibilities

1. Did you plan to use the money primarily to benefit yourself or to help others as well? How does your answer symbolize your values? *Refer to page 134.*

2. What does your answer indicate about your attitude toward money, crises, responsibility, others? Did you take anyone else into account? Did you begin to plan for a way to begin again? *Refer to page 135.*

3. Why did you choose this particular person? (Is it someone you wouldn't dare speak to in that way in reality? Or perhaps a person you've been waiting to get at but haven't had the opportunity?) On reflection, do you like what you had to say? How do you feel after such an exercise (relieved, upset, frustrated)? *Refer to page 136.*

4. Does your answer have any value in suggesting ways of living your life now? Any week may possibly be your last and some week certainly will be. *Refer to page 137.*

DATE_____

5. Can you take steps now to implement your ideas? *Refer to page 138.*

6. Are you willing to make sacrifices to improve your family life? How might you begin right now? *Refer to page 139.*

7. Did you choose wishes for yourself? For others? Did you wish for the kinds of things that are "miraculous" or can they be attained through hard work? Are they the kind of wishes you would be proud to talk about? *Refer to page 140.*

DATE_____

8. Do you have a true desire to simplify your life? What would be the advantages of doing so? Would there be drawbacks? *Refer to page 141.*

IMAGING POSSIBILITIES **283**

9. Is this based on personal experience? Does it say anything about how you treat others, regardless of their age? *Refer to page 142.*

Q. Is this based on personal experience? Does this say anything about how you treat others? Is there some way that you can contribute to the spreading of this idea of yours to influence others? *Refer to page 143.*

11. How do you define success—in terms of possessions, recognition by others, goals achieved, self-satisfaction? What does this reveal about your character? *Refer to page 144.*

2. Evaluate your answer in terms of what you think is the meaning of life. *Refer to page 145.*

DATE_____

13. How do you see your answer in terms of ultimate values and meaning? *Refer to page 146.*

DATE_____

4. Did you describe peace in global terms or personal ones? Does this indicate something about your concerns at this time of your life? *Refer to page 147.*

15. Is this something you feel often—or rarely? *Refer to page 148.*